RENOI

A POSTCARD BOOK™

Running Press
Philadelphia, Pennsylvania

Postcard Book is a trademark of Running Press Book Publishers.

Canadian representatives: General Publishing Co., Ltd., 30 Lesmill Road, Don Mills, Ontario M3B 2T6.
International representatives: Worldwide Media Services, Inc., 115 East Twenty-third Street, New York, New York 10010.

9   8   7
The digit on the right indicates the number of this printing.

ISBN 0-89472-684-0
Cover design by Toby Schmidt.
Cover illustration: *Dinner by the River* (detail), 1879, by Pierre-Auguste Renoir. Photograph: The Granger Collection, New York.
Back cover illustration: *The Theater Box*, 1874, by Pierre-Auguste Renoir. Photograph: Art Resource, New York.
Title page illustration: *At the Moulin de la Galette,* 1876, by Pierre-Auguste Renoir. Photograph: Art Resource, New York.

Typography by COMMCOR Communications Corporation, Philadelphia, Pennsylvania.
Printed and bound in the United States of America by Innovation Printing.
This book may be ordered by mail from the publisher. Please add $2.50 for postage and handling. *But try your bookstore first!*
Running Press Book Publishers, 125 South Twenty-second Street, Philadelphia, Pennsylvania 19103

At the age of 13, Pierre-Auguste Renoir began work in a factory painting delicate flowers onto white porcelain. The son of an obscure Parisian tailor, he was proud of his craft. However, a new mechanical process for stamping patterns on china rendered his skill obsolete four years later. He shifted then to painting ladies' fans, decorating them with pastoral scenes reminiscent of 18th-century paintings by Watteau and Fragonard that he admired while wandering through the Louvre on Sunday afternoons. Studying those paintings made him long to paint larger works himself.

In 1862, at the age of 21, Renoir had saved enough money to study art in the studio of Marc-Gabriel-Charles Gleyre. He learned little from his master, but plenty from the other students—among them Alfred Sisley, Frédéric Bazille, and Claude Monet. When Gleyre retired in 1864, his students were already teaching themselves a new style of painting that would change European art forever.

Leaving the confines of the studio, Renoir and Monet set up their easels outdoors in the countryside, where they experimented with the new theories of art that were being endlessly discussed in Paris's bohemian cafés. Eliminating black and brown from their palettes, they played with the optical effects that other colors had in proximity to each other. By using choppy brushstrokes and a palette knife, they conveyed motion, texture, and the shimmer of sunlight. Influenced especially by Edouard Manet, Renoir and Monet covered large canvases with lively figures pursuing the bourgeois pleasures of cafés, picnics, and dance gardens. Although Renoir had barely enough money to buy paints, he still delighted in creating beautiful pictures that expressed his own easy, joyous appetite for life.

In 1874, Renoir, Monet, and fellow artists Paul Cézanne and Edgar Degas held their first exhibition—in defiance of the influential Paris Salon, which had refused their work. At first, viewers were shocked and disturbed by art so far removed from French classicism. In eight shows over the next 12 years, however, the "Impressionists"—so called for the immediacy and emotion of their work—gained public acceptance.

In 1875, wealthy patrons began to underwrite Renoir's work. In 1876, in a burst of creative activity, Renoir produced such wondrous pictures as *At the Moulin de la Galette.* A trip to Italy in 1881, however, turned him against the "formlessness" of Impressionism, and he gravitated toward more classical subjects, making his figures more solid and adding more yellows and reds to his palette.

When he was in his late fifties, Renoir began suffering from arthritis, which eventually confined him to a wheelchair. Determined to continue painting, he worked by strapping a brush to his crabbed and crippled hand. But after his death in 1919, it became evident that he would always be remembered best for the work he had repudiated, the luminous pictures of his Impressionist years.

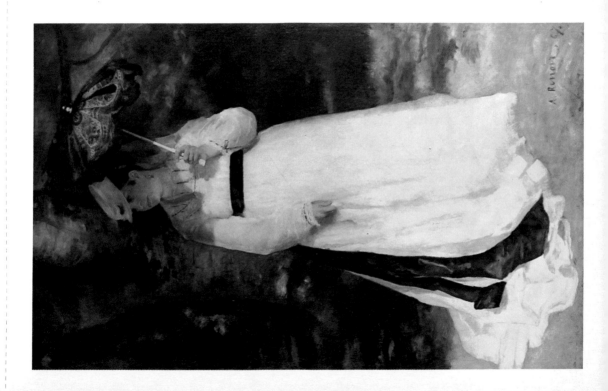

Renoir

LISE

1867, by Pierre-Auguste Renoir (French, 1841–1919). Photograph: The Granger Collection, New York.

RENOIR A Postcard Book™   ©*1989 by Running Press Book Publishers*

Renoir

ODALISQUE

1870, by Pierre-Auguste Renoir (French, 1841–1919). Photograph: The Granger Collection, New York.

RENOIR A Postcard Book™   ©*1989 by Running Press Book Publishers*

Renoir

THE READER

1874, by Pierre-Auguste Renoir (French, 1841–1919). Photograph: The Granger Collection, New York.

RENOIR A Postcard Book™   ©*1989 by Running Press Book Publishers*

Renoir

THE DANCER

1874, by Pierre-Auguste Renoir (French, 1841–1919). Photograph: The Granger Collection, New York.

RENOIR   A Postcard Book™   ©*1989 by Running Press Book Publishers*

Renoir

THE THEATER BOX

1874, by Pierre-Auguste Renoir (French, 1841–1919). Photograph: Art Resource, New York.

RENOIR   A Postcard Book™   ©*1989 by Running Press Book Publishers*

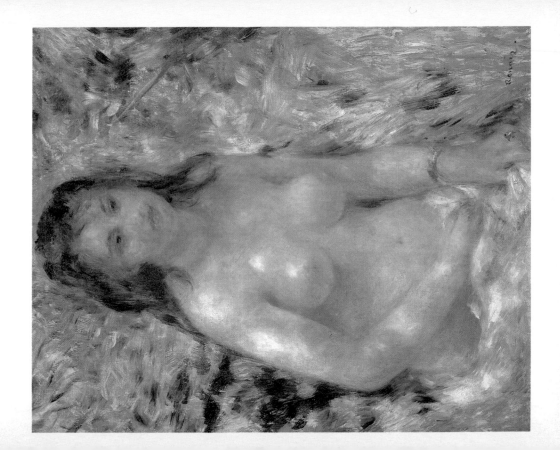

Renoir

TORSO OF A WOMAN IN THE SUN

1876, by Pierre-Auguste Renoir (French, 1841–1919). Photograph: Art Resource, New York.

RENOIR A Postcard Book™   ©*1989 by Running Press Book Publishers*

Renoir

THE SWING

1876, by Pierre-Auguste Renoir (French, 1841–1919). Photograph: The Granger Collection, New York.

RENOIR A Postcard Book™   ©*1989 by Running Press Book Publishers*

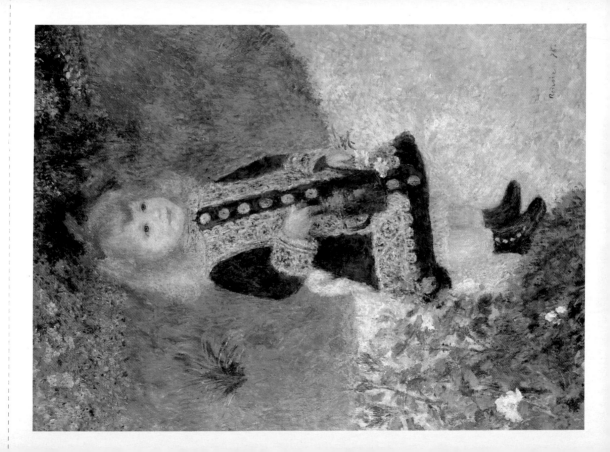

Renoir

GIRL WITH A WATERING CAN

1876, by Pierre-Auguste Renoir (French, 1841–1919). Photograph: Art Resource, New York.

RENOIR A Postcard Book™   ©*1989 by Running Press Book Publishers*

Renoir

AT THE MOULIN DE LA GALETTE

1876, by Pierre-Auguste Renoir (French, 1841–1919). Photograph: Art Resource, New York.

RENOIR A Postcard Book™   ©*1989 by Running Press Book Publishers*

Renoir

MME. CHARPENTIER AND HER CHILDREN

1878, by Pierre-Auguste Renoir (French, 1841–1919). Photograph: The Granger Collection, New York.

RENOIR A Postcard Book™   *©1989 by Running Press Book Publishers*

Renoir

Renoir

TWO LITTLE CIRCUS GIRLS

1879, by Pierre-Auguste Renoir (French, 1841–1919). Photograph: The Granger Collection, New York.

RENOIR A Postcard Book™   *©1989 by Running Press Book Publishers*

Renoir

DINNER BY THE RIVER

1879, by Pierre-Auguste Renoir (French, 1841–1919). Photograph: The Granger Collection, New York.

RENOIR A Postcard Book™   ©*1989 by Running Press Book Publishers*

Renoir

THE UMBRELLAS

1879–1880, by Pierre-Auguste Renoir (French, 1841–1919). Photograph: The Granger Collection, New York.

RENOIR A Postcard Book™   ©*1989 by Running Press Book Publishers*

Renoir

ON THE TERRACE

1881, by Pierre-Auguste Renoir (French, 1841–1919). Photograph: The Granger Collection, New York.

RENOIR A Postcard Book™   ©1989 by *Running Press Book Publishers*

Renoir

SAN MARCO, VENICE

1881, by Pierre-Auguste Renoir (French, 1841–1919). Photograph: The Granger Collection, New York.

RENOIR A Postcard Book™   ©*1989 by Running Press Book Publishers*

Renoir

STILL LIFE WITH PEACHES

1881, by Pierre-Auguste Renoir (French, 1841–1919). Photograph: The Granger Collection, New York.

RENOIR   A Postcard Book™   ©*1989 by Running Press Book Publishers*

Renoir

DANCING IN THE CITY

1883, by Pierre-Auguste Renoir (French, 1841–1919). Photograph: The Granger Collection, New York.

RENOIR A Postcard Book™   ©*1989 by Running Press Book Publishers*

Renoir

DANCING IN THE COUNTRY

1883, by Pierre-Auguste Renoir (French, 1841–1919). Photograph: The Granger Collection: New York.

RENOIR A Postcard Book™   ©*1989 by Running Press Book Publishers*

Renoir

WOMAN SITTING BY THE SEASHORE

1883, by Pierre-Auguste Renoir (French, 1841–1919). Photograph: The Granger Collection, New York.

RENOIR   A Postcard Book™   ©*1989 by Running Press Book Publishers*

Renoir

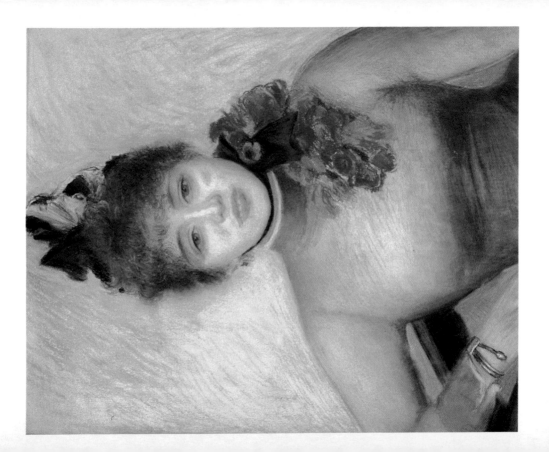

Renoir

Renoir

BATHER ARRANGING HER HAIR

1887, by Pierre-Auguste Renoir (French, 1841–1919). Photograph: The Granger Collection, New York.

RENOIR A Postcard Book™   ©*1989 by Running Press Book Publishers*

Renoir

BATHER SEATED ON A ROCK

1892, by Pierre-Auguste Renoir (French, 1841–1919). Photograph: The Granger Collection, New York.

RENOIR A Postcard Book™   *©1989 by Running Press Book Publishers*

Renoir

YOUNG GIRLS AT A PIANO

c. 1892, by Pierre-Auguste Renoir (French, 1841–1919). Photograph: Art Resource, New York.

RENOIR A Postcard Book™   *©1989 by Running Press Book Publishers*

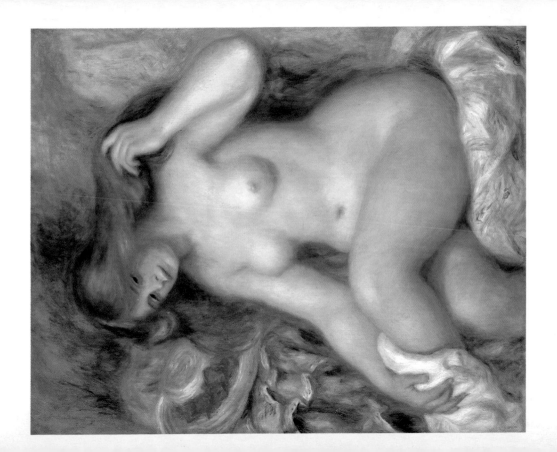

Renoir

BATHER

1903, by Pierre-Auguste Renoir (French, 1841–1919). Photograph: Art Resource, New York.

RENOIR   A Postcard Book™   ©*1989 by Running Press Book Publishers*

Renoir

STRAWBERRIES

c. 1905, by Pierre-Auguste Renoir (French, 1841–1919). Photograph: Art Resource, New York.

RENOIR A Postcard Book™   *©1989 by Running Press Book Publishers*

Renoir

CLAUDE RENOIR WITH TOYS

c. 1906, by Pierre-Auguste Renoir (French, 1841–1919). Photograph: Art Resource, New York.

RENOIR A Postcard Book™   ©*1989 by Running Press Book Publishers*

Renoir

WOMAN TYING HER SHOE

c. 1918, by Pierre-Auguste Renoir (French, 1841–1919). Photograph: The Granger Collection, New York.

RENOIR A Postcard Book™   *©1989 by Running Press Book Publishers*

Renoir

THE BATHERS (DETAIL)

c. 1918, by Pierre-Auguste Renoir (French, 1841–1919). Photograph: The Granger Collection, New York.

RENOIR A Postcard Book™   ©*1989 by Running Press Book Publishers*